# Kid Blink Beats
# *THE WORLD*

DON BROWN

ROARING BROOK PRESS

BROOKFIELD, CONNECTICUT

*For Danny, Nick, Beth, and Thom*

Copyright © 2004 by Don Brown

Published by Roaring Brook Press

Roaring Brook Press is a division of Holtzbrinck Publishing Holdings Limited Partnership

2 Old New Milford Road, Brookfield, Connecticut 06804

Distributed in Canada by H. B. Fenn and Company Ltd.

Library of Congress Cataloging-in-Publication Data

Brown, Don, 1949-

Kid blink beats the world / by Don Brown.—1st ed.

p.   cm.

Summary: A story of the newsboys (and girls) who took on the world's most powerful press barons—and won.

1. Newspaper vendors—New York—New York City—History—19th century. 2. Strikes and lockouts—Newspapers—New York—New York City—

History—19th century. 3. Child labor—New York—New York City—History—19th century. [1. Newspaper carriers. 2. Newspaper publishing. 3.

Newspapers—History—19th century. 4. Strikers and lockouts. 5. Child labor. 6. New York (N.Y.)—History—19th century.] I. Title.

HD8039.N42U63 2004          331.3¢18—dc22

2003021896

ISBN 1-59643-003-6

Roaring Brook Press books are available for special promotions and premiums.

For details contact: Director of Special Markets, Holtzbrinck Publishers.

First edition September 2004

Book design by Jennifer Browne

Printed in the United States of America

2  4  6  8  10  9  7  5  3  1

It was all for a penny.

They left their cramped and crowded tenement apartments for a penny.

They scurried beside the pushcart peddlers for a penny.

They dodged street trolleys and horse drawn wagons for a penny.

And in the summer of 1899, Kid Blink, Race Track Higgins, Tiny Tim, Crutch Morris, and Crazy Arborn battled the world for a penny.

The boys were newsies. They and thousands of youngsters like them peddled *The World* and *The Journal* newspapers on the streets of New York City, a penny a paper.

They bought stacks of papers, five cents for every ten copies, and then hawked them to passersby. The trick was to sell them all and not to be left with unsold papers.

"Extra! Extra! Read all about it! Ship sinks! Bridge collapses! Building burns!" they yelled, trying to capture the curiosity of anyone listening. Sometimes they invented their own headlines when the real thing was dull.

At the end of the day and scores of sold copies later, a newsie might have made twenty-five cents, a generous wage in a time when a family survived on ten dollars a week and fifteen cents fetched a dinner of soup, stew, and pie.

But then two of the most popular papers, *The World* and *The Journal*, demanded that the newsies pay more for their stacks, *six cents* for ten papers. Their powerful owners, Mr. Pulitzer and Mr. Hearst, reckoned by doing so they could wring more money from their businesses and for themselves. And in the end, making more money was the object of their labors.

But the penny difference angered the newsies, for they understood that an extra penny for the newspapers was a penny lost to them.

"Ten cents in a dollar is as much to us as it is to Hearst and Pulitzer who are millionaires. . . . I'm trying to figure how ten cents on a hundred papers can mean more to a millionaire than it does to newsboys, an' I can't see it," Kid Blink explained. "If they can't spare it, how can we?"

It was only a penny but the young boys and girls wouldn't have it. So they decided to strike and stop all sales of *The World* and *The Journal* until the price was rolled back.

Three hundred newsies rallied on July 20th near the newspapers' offices in lower Manhattan, and tried to halt delivery of the papers. But the police scattered the youngsters, took a few to jail, and the papers got out. Still, kindhearted onlookers showed their support and rained coins on the youngsters from overlooking windows.

The bosses of *The World* ignored the demands of the youthful news peddlers.

"We have the situation well in hand," they said.

But uptown, hundreds of newsies heard of the strike. They decorated lampposts with banners that read "Please Don't Buy *The World* and *The Journal*," "Our Cause Is Just," and "We Will Fight For Our Rights." When the newspaper delivery wagons arrived, newsies surrounded them and, with hoots and howls, drove off the deliverymen and trampled the newspapers.

THE WORLD

That night Kid Blink told a mob of newsies, "The time has come when we must either make a stand or be down ridden by the disciples of avarice and greediness. Is you all still with us in the cause?"

"Sure! Sure!" the crowd cheered.

The next day newsies wore signs in their hats and handed out leaflets begging people not to buy *The World* and *The Journal*.

They stopped newspaper deliveries,

pummeled deliverymen
with rotten fruit,

and swiped papers from
the few kids and newsstands
that still sold the papers.

The strike dented the newspaper bosses' confidence.

"The people seem to be against us; they are encouraging the boys and tipping them," the bosses said.

Even though newsies like Abe Greenhouse, Joe Mulligan, and Donato Caroluci were arrested, the strikers didn't lose heart. Tiny Tim, a young news seller from 23rd Street, was asked how long the strikers could hold out.

*"Ferever,"* he said.

Harlem, Brooklyn, and Staten Island newsies joined the strike, as did those in Newark and Jersey City, New Jersey. The strikers planned a huge parade across the Brooklyn Bridge, and Race Track Higgins visited Chief of Police Devery for a permit.

"Go away, you slob," the Chief said.

"Mr. Devery, don't call me a slob. I'm trying to make my living. I ain't so high in office as you, but some day I may be higher," Race Track replied.

But the Chief was unmoved and the parade plan was squashed. Instead, on the evening of July 24th the newsies gathered at New Irving Hall on Broome Street, a neighborhood of tenements teeming with immigrant families, a neighborhood said to be the most crowded on earth. Five thousand newsies, many of them the children of those immigrants, filled the hall and swarmed the street outside. Crazy Arborn brought 1,500 pretzels.

There were mad cheers and shouts for order. Visiting politicians applauded the strike. Newsies made speeches of encouragement.

"Just stick together and we'll win. Is it boys?" Kid Blink asked the horde.

"It is!" they shouted back.

"Now, you all know me, boys, don't you?"

"We do! We do!"

"Well, we'll all go out tomorrow and stick together, and we'll win a walk," he said and the crowd awarded him a giant flower horseshoe for his speech.

The strike pressed on. Newsies skirmished with thugs and toughs hired by the newspaper bosses to sell papers and frighten the strikers.

Beside the Brooklyn Bridge, they caught a woman selling papers from her newsstand. Many of the newsies wanted to swipe her copies, but Kid Blink stopped them.

"A feller don't soak a lady," he explained.

They raided news wagons and the papers were left in tatters. One downtown street was left awash in six inches of torn papers.

Permit or not, they paraded up the avenues in the hundreds.
The police arrived and they escaped down alleys or
disappeared among the street peddlers. Still,
Frank Desso, Cornelius Boyle,
and Isaac Miller went to jail.

But the strike pinched newspaper sales and the bosses moaned that their losses were "colossal" and "appalling."

Newsies in Rochester, Troy, and Yonkers New York; Newark, Trenton, and Paterson, New Jersey; Providence, Rhode Island; New Haven, Connecticut; Fall River, Massachusetts; Cincinnati, Ohio; Lexington, Kentucky joined the strike. Messenger boys and shoe shine boys joined the strike in sympathy.

In less than two weeks, nearly all the newsies in New York City and adjacent towns had quit selling papers. Where once the papers were printing 350,000 copies a day, they now printed only 125,000.

The newsies had won!

But the unlikely strike had an unlikely ending.

*The World* and *The Journal* didn't lower their price. Instead, they offered to buy back all copies of the newspaper the newsies were unable to sell. It was neither victory nor defeat but something in between, a compromise.

Clustered on the pushcart crowded streets, beside the trolleys and horse drawn wagons, and in the shadow of the cramped tenements, the newsies tallied the gains and losses the compromise offered. When their calculations pointed to more money in their pockets, they decided to accept the deal. For in the end, the newsies were no different than Mr. Pulitzer and Mr. Hearst; more money was the object of *their* labors, too. And the newsies knew that more pennies in their pockets meant more pennies for their families and a better life for them all.

And wasn't that what it was all for?

# Author's Note

*The World* and *The Journal*'s plan to squeeze pennies from the newsies wasn't adopted by the city's other papers. *The New York Times* and *The New York Tribune*, for example, left their prices unchanged and were not struck. It is these papers' strike coverage that provide us with the record of the newsies struggle. Undoubtedly happy to enlarge upon their competitors' discomfort, the other newspapers portrayed the newsies as urban Peter Pans and Robin Hoods, endearing urchins who delivered mock-heroic speeches in dialects-ridden, fractured English. "Me men is nobul," Kid Blink is reported to have said. "And wid such as dese to oppose der neferarious schemes how can de blokes hope to win?" (Kid Blink was a popular subject of the press and appeared in many newspaper stories. Reported to be blind in one eye, the papers sometimes referred to him as "Mr. Blink.") Still, news stories rife with "dem," "dese," and "doz" must have irked the newsies; at the New Irving Hall rally they told the papers to cut it out. And in spite of the patronizing, whimsical nature of much of the news coverage, the reality of the strike must have been more sobering. The newsies were largely poor, many from immigrant families in New York's tenement neighborhoods. The pennies the strikers earned wasn't a trifle intended for their own amusement but an essential contribution to their families' existence; the loss of even a single penny was intolerable. The strike was violent: the newspapers hired men to protect the newspaper deliveries and there were fights using fists and clubs and reports of threats involving revolvers.

And what became of Kid Blink, Crazy Arborn, Race Track Higgins, Barney Peanuts, Jim Gaiety and the rest at the conclusion of the strike? They slipped back into obscurity and anonymously made their way into the Twentieth Century, where two World Wars, the Great Depression, and the Nuclear Age awaited them.

## Bibliography

Burrows, Edwin G. and Wallace, Mike, *Gotham, A History of New York City to 1898*. New York: Oxford University Press, 1999.

Marx, Harpo, *Harpo Speaks . . . about New York*. New York: The Little Book Room, 1961

Nasaw, David, *Children of the City*. Garden City: Anchor Press/Doubleday, 1985.

*The New York Times*, July 21-August 2, 1899.

*New York Tribune*, July 21-August 2, 1899.

Riis, Jacob, *How The Other Half Lives* (1901). Reprinted, New York: Dover Publications, 1971.

# DATE DUE

| | | | |
|---|---|---|---|
| | | | |
| | | | |
| | | | |
| | | | |
| | | | |
| | | | |
| | | | |
| | | | |
| | | | |
| | | | |
| | | | |
| | | | |
| | | | |

THE LIBRARY STORE  #47-0204